The World Book Library of Wildlife

A Chanticleer Press Edition
Although this book was previously published as part of
The Audubon Society Book of Wild Animals, *this edition is sponsored*
exclusively by World Book-Childcraft International, Inc.

The World Book of Elephants, Zebras and Other Plant Eaters

by Les Line and Edward Ricciuti

World Book-Childcraft International, Inc.

A Subsidiary of the Scott & Fetzer Company
Chicago   London   Sydney   Tokyo   Toronto

Library of Congress Cataloging in Publication data:
Line, Les
The World Book of Elephants, Zebras and Other Plant Eaters.
"A Chanticleer Press edition."

ISBN 0-7166-2302-X (volume 3)
World Book Library of Wildlife ISBN 0-7166-2300-5 (the set)
Library of Congress Catalog Card Number: 81-52954

Originally published in 1977 by Harry N. Abrams, Incorporated,
New York, as part of *The Audubon Society Book of Wild Animals*.

Prepared and produced by Chanticleer Press, Inc.
Printed in the United States.

Cover photograph by Jon A. Hull/Bruce Coleman, Inc.

*Note on Illustration Numbers: All illustrations are numbered
according to the pages on which they appear.*

First frontispiece. *An American bison* (Bison bison) *is silhouetted by
the morning sun on the prairie of South Dakota.* (ANIMALS ANIMALS/
© Mark Newman)

Second frontispiece. *Armed with scimitar-shaped horns that may exceed
five feet in length, the sable antelope* (Hippotragus niger) *fears not even
a circling pride of lions. Herds of up to eighty sables—rust-colored
females, their young, and one jet-black old bull—roam the woodland
savannas of southern Africa.* (Thomas Nebbia)

Contents

When the Prophet Isaiah said "All flesh is grass," he anticipated by many centuries one of the basic truths of present-day ecology. We now know that all animal life is completely dependent upon plants for its existence. All but a minute amount of the energy used by living things comes from the sun, and only plants, by means of the process of photosynthesis, can capture this energy and use it to combine water and carbon dioxide to form simple sugars and other substances necessary for life. In building these basic substances, plants draw potassium, calcium, iron, and other elements from the soil. Plants are the sole source of energy and nutrients in the ecosystem.

As nutrients and solar energy move upward in the food-chain, from plant to plant eater to predator, the supply diminishes at each step. When a plant-eating animal, or herbivore, feeds on a plant, much of the energy contained in it is lost as heat. The same is true when a predator feeds on an herbivore; much of the energy is lost, and only a small fraction of it goes to sustain the life of the predator.

For the rich variety of plant-eating mammals in this book, this simple matter of energy has profound implications. The steady decrease in available energy at each step in the food-chain is reflected in a similar decrease in the *biomass*, or total weight of living substance. One hundred tons of plant tissue might support ten tons of herbivores, and one ton of predators. With the greatest amount of energy at their disposal and the largest biomass, the herbivores are the basic group of animals in the food-chain, and have the largest populations. It is no accident that many of the world's

Foreword

greatest wildlife spectacles have involved the plant-eating mammals—the millions of bison that once roamed the North American plains, the great herds of zebras and wildebeests that move across the grasslands of East Africa, or the stirring migrations of the caribou in the Canadian Arctic.

Not all herbivores build up populations as great as these. Deer and other browsers may be thinly distributed through the forest, and the plant eaters of the deserts and high mountains, where there is little vegetation, may also be correspondingly scarce. But they are always more numerous than the predators that stalk them. We usually think of antelope, deer, and other grazing and browsing mammals as leading perilous lives, surrounded by an ever-present threat from the flesh eaters. But in a way, it is the predators that are most vulnerable. With their numbers kept permanently small by the limited amount of energy available to them, they are as dependent on the herbivores as the herbivores are on plants. Without the plant eaters described and pictured in this book, animals able to make use of the solar energy and nutrients contained in plants, there would be no predators at all.

Lying in the snows of January, an antler discarded by a whitetail buck affirms the continuity of nature, the marvelous cycle of life that progresses unbroken through the endless round of seasons. Crusted with ice, perhaps, or gnawed by rodents, the jettisoned tree of bone on the woodland floor promises new life to come from old, but at the same time cautions that certain variations in the way the pledge is fulfilled may elude human understanding. Antlers are the peculiar property of the deer family, half a hundred species of generally graceful cud chewers native to the Americas, Eurasia, some large Far Eastern islands, and northwestern Africa, and widely introduced beyond those areas. Although sometimes used as a weapon, the primary role of antlers is sexual, because ultimately they expedite the inheritance by the young of genes rich in survival value. The sexual import of antlers is signified by the fact that they are carried only by the males and employed in bruising tournaments to gain dominance and the right to mate with females. There are exceptions to the all-male rule. Both sexes of the Eurasian reindeer *(Rangifer tarandus)* and its North American counterpart, the caribou, carry antlers. However, antlers are entirely missing from either sex of two Asian species, the Chinese water deer *(Hydropotes inermis)*, which has been introduced into England, and the small musk deer *(Moschus moschiferus)*. Instead, the two Asian deer have sharp canine tusks in the upper jaw. Oddities today, they may resemble the creatures from which the deer tribe arose, for the ancestors of the deer showed no sign of antlers. During the past 25 million years or so,

The Deer Tribe

however, antlers have appeared and evolved into myriad sizes and configurations. The smallest deer, the foot-high pudus *(Pudu)* of South America, and the largest, the hulking, 1800-pound moose *(Alces alces)* of North America and Eurasia, also stand at opposite ends of size when it comes to antlers. Those of the pudus are slender, finger-length spikes. The moose carries massive, palmate antlers that have a spread of more than six feet and outweigh the entire body of the twenty-pound pudu by a factor of five. The giant stag, or "Irish elk," which strode across the open landscape of Europe during the last ice age, had antlers that spanned nine feet and weighed about 150 pounds.

Changes in the antlers as they bud, grow, and eventually deteriorate mirror changes in the life of the deer as they move through their yearly reproductive cycle. Shedding of the antlers signals that mating is past, that males may join one another or on occasion even mix with the females without conflict or sexual involvement. The Eurasian roe deer *(Capreolus capreolus)* mates in summer and sheds in autumn. The Père David's deer *(Elaphurus davidianus)* of China, extinct as a wild animal for centuries but preserved in zoos, follows a similar cycle. The American whitetail *(Odocoileus virginianus)*, which ranges in size from more than 300 pounds in the North to a 50-pound race of midgets in the Florida Keys, mates in autumn and is without its antlers by midwinter. The gorgeously spotted axis deer *(Axis axis)* of India and Sri Lanka usually mates in the spring, and when it does, drops its antlers in August. But axis deer have also been known to mate at any time of the year, and shed in corresponding fashion, a situation rather typical of tropical deer. For example, the big swamp deer *(Blastocerus dichotomus)* and the pampas deer *(Ozotoceras campestris)* of South America lose their antlers at odd times of the year, and coincidentally have no regular breeding season. Nor do the males of these species engage in rutting battles. Reportedly, the same is true of stags of the sleek Asian barasingha *(Cervus duvaucelli)*; their antlers are still encased in a coat of velvet at breeding time.

For most deer, however, the rutting season opens just as the antlers become gleaming hard. Their maturation heralds the beginning of competition between the males, a contest that may be waged at levels of which we are oblivious. The antlers almost certainly express the dominance of the fittest males in more subtle ways. A splendid set of antlers unquestionably advertises the vitality of its owner, and indeed, the growth of antlers is intimately linked to the production of the male hormone testosterone. A stag that is neutered while it is immature, and thus deprived of testosterone, never produces antlers. A spayed female injected with it develops a rudimentary set of antlers.

Mature antler is bone which has grown rapidly out of the skull and then died. No other bone grows so profusely after birth, and the accelerated buildup of cells as the antler develops has been likened to the runaway multiplication of bone cancer cells, but with the control and direction needed to form a precise structure. While growing, the antler is linked internally to the blood supply of the skull. As the bone hardens, the linkage is carried out through vessels in the velvet, the tender skin over the growing antler. Eventually, as hormones ebb and flow in the body, the blood supply dwindles, and the velvet shrivels, frays, and is rubbed off on trees and other objects.

When their antlers are polished and ready, the males, which generally have lived by themselves for several months, roam in search of females. Most male deer announce their readiness to mate—and to do battle—with challenging calls that blast over the landscape. The moose emits a raspy roar. The North American mule deer *(Odocoileus hemionus)* gives out loud grunts.

The graceful fallow deer *(Dama dama)*, introduced to Europe from the Middle East as early as classical times, coughs. The sika deer *(Cervus nippon)* of Asia utters shrill, piercing sounds. The most explosive calls of all, however, come from the European red deer *(C. elaphus)*, and especially its North American relative the elk *(C. elaphus)*.

The red deer, fabled stag of medieval legend and lore, and of the golden artwork of the Scythians, challenges with a harsh, grating bellow that leaves little doubt it means business. The bugle of the elk is one of the most thrilling sounds in the animal kingdom, as during September and October the valleys of the Rocky Mountains and a few other havens left to the creatures echo to their calls. Muzzles lifted to the sky, antlers tilted back on necks swollen with blood, the bulls scream clarion clear. The mere bugle of a big bull can send a rival fleeing. Elk and, in fact, other deer in rut can be lethal creatures as they walk stiff-legged in search of competitors.

There comes a time, however, when males of equivalent size and strength clash. Elk and moose pairs come together with head-shattering clashes. Whitetails and mule deer fence close up, pushing and shoving. Sometimes one is killed or injured, but usually the weaker backs off. One of the few deer that seemingly fights to kill in rutting bouts is the hog deer *(Axis porcinus)* of Asia, which charges with antlers canted to the side so the points reach the opponent's body rather than engage his tines. Once the branching structures of deer antlers engage those of an opponent, the sharp points of the tines usually are kept at a distance. The greatest danger to the combatants is that the antlers will lock, leaving them to slow, grim death by starvation.

The antlers are seldom used for fighting predators, and for that matter are either absent or absolutely useless most of the year. Most deer box enemies with their razor-sharp hooves. Whitetail deer kill snakes by stamping upon them. A moose can break the skull of a wolf or a bear with a swipe of its huge front hooves. Male deer that triumph in mating battles often gather large harems about them. Caribou and reindeer bulls may have up to forty cows, some with their young. Mule deer are somewhat lackadaisical, and gather only three or four females, which are allowed to wander off. Moose often remain with one cow, but also sometimes spread their attention among several. The roe deer buck fixes his desire on only one female, which he pursues in long chases over the countryside. Often the pursuit takes the shape of a small circle, which the deer tread into fields and meadows. The imprint of their revels is the so-called witch circle of European lore. Once mating is complete, male deer leave the females. Often the males remain in bachelor herds until the next rut approaches, but sometimes, especially in winter, deer will form loose herds of both sexes.

With the end of breeding, the antler loses its purpose. Ironically, it is cast off because it starts to grow again. The spurt of new growth occurs on the frontal bones of the skull, in the bony platform from which the antler arose. The antler, however, is dead, and cannot respond to growth, so the force of new cells piling up below pushes it up and away from the skull, until it is so loosely joined that a casual blow, or even a vigorous shake of the head, will dislodge it. Fallen to the ground, the antler is a silent message declaring that nature regenerates itself even as it dies.

13. *Late-afternoon sun highlights the budding, velvet-covered antlers and outsized ears of a mule deer* (Odocoileus hemionus), *the deer of mountains and deserts of western North America. Mule deer are noted for the strange way they run in flight, bounding in four-foot-high leaps, looking backward each time to check on their pursuer. In some areas, local people call it the jumping deer. Mule deer are plagued in summer with ticks—thousands of them on a single animal—and, like the oxpeckers that accompany the wild buffalo of Africa, magpies and jays will perch on a deer's back and pluck off the pests. Occasionally one deer will chew at the parasites on another deer. Black bears and the rare grizzly prey heavily on mule deer fawns, and coyotes will try to bring down an adult, but more often than not it will be routed or killed by flailing hooves. The mule deer's big eyes give it superb vision in the dim light of dawn and dusk.* (Bob and Jill Stoecker/Natura Photographica)

14. *A month after its birth in late June, a mule deer fawn can keep pace with its mother as she moves about their home range of about a square mile. Though the fawn is still nursing, it begins to sample the mule deer's varied diet of foliage of all kinds of mountain shrubs and trees and abundant summer mushrooms. By the time the fawn is weaned in September, its spotted coat has been replaced by one of long, heavy hair. This shaggy winter coat is noted only on first-year deer, who are facing the most critical season of their lives.* (ANIMALS ANIMALS/© Mark Stouffer)

15 *top. Except for its long antlers and a bushy tail, the hog deer* (Axis porcinus) *of India and Southeast Asia indeed does resemble a pig: it is squat, stocky, and has a piglike gait when it runs across the grasslands.* (Thase Daniel)

15 *bottom. Lacking antlers, the male musk deer* (Moschus moschiferus) *instead has canine tusks that jut three inches below its jaws. This small, timid deer of central and northeastern Asia is relentlessly hunted for the musk gland of the male, because the small quantity of musk it contains is in great demand for perfumes and soaps. Countless females and young also perish in traps set by native hunters.* (Belinda Wright)

16 *overleaf. The spotted red coat of the axis deer or chital* (Axis axis) *adds color and beauty to the grasslands of India and Sri Lanka. Of all Asiatic deer, this is the most gregarious, forming herds of males, females, and young that number more than one hundred.* (Belinda Wright)

18. *Antlers of the sambar* (Cervus unicolor) *of southern Asia uniformly have only six tines, a fact noted by Alexander the Great on his campaign in northern India in 326* B.C. *and subsequently recorded by the Greek philosopher and zoologist Aristotle. Thus this large but stealthy deer of bamboo jungles and dense forests is sometimes called Aristotle's deer.* (Jean-Paul Ferrero)

19. *New antlers are growing on an axis deer. Like all deer of tropical regions, axis stags shed their antlers irregularly, during all months of the year. Antlerless stags form all-male herds, an individual returning to the mixed herd when a replacement set is fully formed.* (Stanley Breeden)

20 *overleaf. A flashing white "flag" disappearing into the dense forest is often a hiker's only clue that he has startled a white-tailed deer* (Odocoileus virginianus) *into flight. The large, waving tail is a signal that helps to keep small groups of this common New World deer together in heavy cover.* (ANIMALS ANIMALS/© Gary Griffen)

22 *second overleaf. During the rut of autumn, as dusk approaches in the national parks of the Rocky Mountains, American elk or wapiti* (Cervus elaphus) *leave the forests for grassy meadows. There, announc-ing his claim to a harem of cows, a bull elk will bugle a long, echoing, three-note call. If he is challenged by a rival, a violent battle is soon to erupt, the two bulls charging from thirty paces and colliding with incredible force. On rare occasions the antlers of two bulls will become inextricably locked together; the combatants are then doomed to death, and the cows over which they fought will be ruled by a lesser bull who was an onlooker at the fatal fight.* (Dean Krakel II)

19

26 *overleaf. It is autumn on the Alaska tundra, and shreds of velvet hang from the tender, blood-red antlers of a bull caribou* (Rangifer tarandus). *The caribou herds have formed up for the migration to their winter range, and a large bull like this will have stored up fifty pounds of fat on its back and rump in preparation for the forthcoming battles of the rutting season. Scraped clean and polished against willows and spruce, the antlers will be put to hard use before they are shed as the heavy snows fall.* (Helen Rhode)

24-25. *The world's largest deer, the moose* (Alces alces) *is a giant resident of marshy forests around the Northern Hemisphere, browsing willows and poplars or wading into ponds and streams to feast on aquatic vegetation, submerging its head—and sometimes its entire massive body—to reach roots and stems. A bull moose, with flat, palmate antlers that spread seventy inches, can weigh 1800 pounds.* (24 Charlie Ott/National Audubon Society Collection/Photo Researchers, Inc.; 25 John Burnley/National Audubon Society Collection/Photo Researchers, Inc.)

Hours before the fall of night, the savanna has been darkened, not by shadows but by the slate-colored forms of the wildebeest, immense herds of them arriving from the dry lands to the south. Leaving the dusty expanses of the Serengeti Plain to the gazelles and ostriches, the wildebeest have made their annual flight from drought. When night finally does cloak the landscape, the air is heavy with the presence of the herds, with a great but muffled stirring of bodies, punctuated by breathy snorts and occasional braying.

The migration of the Serengeti wildebeest *(Connochaetes taurinus)* echoes the mass movements of the enormous herds of hoofed herbivores that once occurred throughout the vast plains of Africa, Eurasia, and North America. These open grasslands have for millennia been the home of multitudes of grazing or browsing creatures, chiefly antelopes, wild cattle, and their relatives. Some of these animals, such as the wisent *(Bison bonasus)* of Europe and the bushbuck *(Tragelaphus scriptus)*, live in the forests, but for millennia the vast herds have inhabited places of far horizons. Today, many of the herds have vanished, or are irreversibly diminished, and few range as freely as in the past. Even so, there are places such as the Serengeti where the herding beasts live much as before, their existence governed by an endless round of different living patterns, repetitive but transitory, distinctly observable but meaningless when separated from the cycle.

For the wildebeest—and until a century ago for the American bison *(Bison bison)*—one of the patterns of life is a seasonal change in range, accomplished by a

Grazing Herds

migratory trek. But for all the horned herds, the cycle of nature's year causes changes that shape their lives even more profoundly than a seasonal shift of scene. Entire animal societies, unshakably stable part of the year, break down and are restructured. The behavior of individuals may change so drastically that they act like entirely new forms of animals. For instance, the male Grant's gazelle *(Gazella granti)* or the hartebeest *(Alcelaphus buselaphus)* that has lived peaceably with others of its sex for months suddenly becomes solitary and cantankerous. The bull African buffalo *(Syncerus caffer)* which has lived on the fringes of the herd becomes gregarious. The female greater kudu *(Tragelaphus strepsiceros)* which has discouraged the approach of bulls with solid butts changes tack and allows a big bull to sidle up alongside her. The timing of such changes of pattern is geared to the survival of the species and of individuals. Correlated to conditions in the environment, the timetable promotes breeding by the adults that are the most fit, the birth of the young when life is easiest, and maximum use of food when it is scarce.

The key to the entire cycle is often the territorial behavior of the males. Among the herds, it varies considerably among species, and even individuals, in the amount of territory claimed and how long it is held, and even whether or not they hold territory. Generally, however, territoriality is strongest when the land is lush, weakest during periods when animals are hard-pressed just to stay alive.

This is dramatically demonstrated by the impala

(Aepyceros melampus), a medium-sized African antelope. At the beginning of the rainy season, when pasturage is rich, the dominant males stake out their territories, about 500 square yards each. The claims are marked with urine, feces, and an oily substance secreted by glands and rubbed onto bushes. The territorial males are easily picked out by the way they stand on their ground—tall and erect, as befits rulers. For up to three months, each male holds his territory against other adult males that seek to take it. Roaring fiercely to proclaim his dominance, the ruler of a particular chunk of territory is kept busy rushing back and forth to check on the small bands of young, non-territorial bachelor males that sometimes wander through his area, and driving off serious challengers. He may dash after an interloper, engage in a fencing match, using his lyre-shaped horns, then turn to meet the next challenger. The loser of the contest ceases territorial behavior and joins the bachelor band. Before becoming a challenger for territory again he must work his way up through the ranks of dominance within the bachelor herd.

Once a male has established a territory, and as long as he holds it, he has the sole right to mate with the groups of females that wander into it in quest of food. When the territorial male is not trying to ward off rivals, he is intent on holding the females in his space and mating with those that are receptive. The females are rather fickle, and males that have the best pasturage in their territories retain the females the longest. An ample supply of food near at hand is also a tremendous advantage for the male as well, because between defending his land and winning the favor of females he has little time to feed. By the end of his tenure his condition deteriorates and he is vulnerable to dispossession by males that were no match for him earlier. The withering of the food supply as the dry season approaches sends the males farther and farther away from their little kingdoms in search of something to eat. Boundaries between the claims are crossed with increasing frequency as the food dwindles and self-preservation replaces the reproductive urges. The dominant males lose interest in maintaining their realms. Eventually, especially if the drought is severe, all defense is abandoned and the territorial system evaporates, as though carried away by the wind that whistles dryly through the acacia thorns. No longer are the various sexual groups of impala kept apart by the domineering rulers of the territories. The antelopes—females, bachelors, and the deposed rulers—mix and focus their energies upon the desperate task of finding food and water on the sun-baked plains.

For most of the herding, hoofed multitudes, the onset of hostile environmental conditions is followed by the disappearance of territorial behavior, a lowering of aggression, and the urge to gather with others of their kind. It happens to the huge gaurs *(Bos gaurus)* of southern Asia during particularly severe droughts, and to the African buffaloes, which gather on the sides of hills and valleys when the dust devils swirl over the landscape. When the rains cease in East Africa, the Thomson's gazelles *(Gazella thomsoni)*, which have been fiercely territorial, herd and migrate from the open plains to the bush in search of fresh pastures and water. On the steppes of Eurasia, the coming of winter ends the vicious territorial combats of the male saiga antelopes *(Saiga tatarica)*. The bulbous-nosed saigas merge into immense herds that run before the wind when blizzards sweep down from Siberia.

Only with the disappearance of territoriality can creatures such as the saigas form great, mixed herds. When the wildebeests migrate, for instance, males inspired by the territorial urge leave the main herds for a day or so, establish their transitory rule, mate with whatever females the can corral, and then return to the main body of antelopes. In contrast, the plains zebra *(Equus burchelli)*, which often travels with the wildebeest and is dependent upon the same pastures, maintains a form of society that does not change with shifting environmental conditions. For the zebra, survival is best served by living year round in small family groups dominated by a king stallion, although stallions also live together in bachelor groups.

For the creatures such as the impala and hartebeest, the cyclic phenomenon of territoriality assures that the bulk of the young will be sired by the finest of the males and that the offspring will be born at a time when their chances of survival are highest. This is accomplished by a marvelous natural synchronization between the time when the dominant males mate, the length of the gestation period, and the onset of the rains, when the land is lush and productive. It is all timed so that the young conceived at the height of the mating season will appear when there is plenty of pasturage, first for their mothers, who consequently can supply sufficient milk, and later for the newly weaned offspring. Moreover, having large numbers of young born at the same time guarantees that a sizable proportion will survive the ravages of predators, which, after all, kill just enough to satisfy their own needs. The young born late, however, have considerably less chance of surviving, not only because of a depleted food supply but also because the predators, no longer luxuriating in an overabundance of prey, pick them off one at a time. Brutally efficient, the system nevertheless works out for the best interests of all species concerned, for the latecomers among the young are often the offspring of less fit males, which have managed to mate at the end of the territorial season, by chance or because the dominant males are through.

33 and **34** overleaf. Whether a solitary bull sharply outlined by the morning sun on the South Dakota prairie, or a herd huddled against pelting snow and subzero cold, the American bison (Bison bison) is a living legend—and a reminder of how close we came to a great tragedy. Once there were 50 million bison on the Great Plains; by 1889, when the market hunters gave up their notorious slaughter, only 541 animals remained! An aroused public succeeded in protecting the survivors, and today there are 25,000 American bison roaming semi-free in the large national parks and wildlife refuges that preserve parts of their historic range. This is the largest land mammal in the New World; a bull, standing five feet at the shoulders, can weigh 2000 pounds. (33 ANIMALS ANIMALS/ © Mark Newman; 34 Steven C. Wilson/Entheos)

36 second overleaf. Sharing the North American plains with the bison when the white man pushed into the western frontier were an estimated 40 million pronghorns (Antilocapra americana). They were not in competition for forage: bison graze the grasses, pronghorns browse shrubs and weeds. Nor did they deplete their pastures, for both species are nomads. There is no faster animal in the New World than the pronghorn: it can maintain a cruising speed of 30 miles an hour over several miles, with bursts up to 40 miles an hour. But it is unable to jump man's barbed-wire fences, and when the wild grasslands were claimed for cattle, the pronghorn population plummeted, reaching a low of 30,000 in the 1920s. Conservation measures have restored pronghorn numbers somewhat, but even so they amount to only one percent of the size of the historic herds. The pronghorn's horn is unique in the mammal kingdom: the bony permanent core is covered with a hard sheath of fused hairs that is shed annually and consumed by rodents. (Steven C. Wilson/Entheos)

38. *The national symbol of South Africa, the springbuck (*Antidorcas marsupialis*) is named for the peculiar way it jumps, or stots, when excited. Holding its legs stiff and its hooves together, the springbuck bounces vertically like a child on a pogo stick, a pouch of white hairs opening on its arched back and flashing at the peak of its ten-foot leaps. One "pronking" springbuck is likely to start an entire herd bouncing.*

Herds of hundreds of thousands of springbucks once migrated across the dry grasslands, but they were decimated late in the nineteenth century by colonists attempting to protect their crops and by a great rinderpest epidemic in 1896. (M. Philip Kahl)

39. *The word "gazelle" is synonymous with grace, delicacy, and beauty, and Grant's gazelle (*Gazella granti*), seen in large numbers on the open plains of East Africa in the company of herds of zebras and wildebeests, is no exception. Male gazelles of varying ages form bachelor herds, but individuals constantly challenge the domination of the buck overseeing a nearby herd of females and young. Grant's gazelles are a common prey of lions, cheetahs, wild dogs, and hyenas.* (Russ Kinne/National Audubon Society Collection/Photo Researchers, Inc.)

40 *overleaf. A water hole in Natal reflects the beauty of a group of female nyalas (*Tragelaphus angasi*). In strange contrast to the hornless female, the bull nyala has twisted horns and a shaggy blue-black coat with a ridge of white hairs down the center of its back. One of the loveliest of all antelopes, the nyala is restricted to the almost impenetrable lowland brush country of southeastern Africa, almost entirely in Mozambique.* (Kenneth B. Newman/Natural History Photographic Agency)

42. *Both male and female oryx* (Oryx gazella) *sport ringed, rapier-like horns, and those of the female are the longer, jutting up to four feet. If attacked by a lion, the oryx lowers its head and directs its menacing weapons forward; but in rutting season, fighting bulls only butt their heads, their horns carefully arranged to avoid injury. So sharp are the horns of this large, beautifully marked antelope—scattered about Africa and Arabia in several subspecies—that natives use the tips as spear points.* (Francisco Erize/Bruce Coleman, Inc.)

43. *The kob* (Kobus kob) *inhabits open grasslands of central Africa near swamps and rivers into which it can retreat to escape midday heat. Herds of kobs establish breeding arenas, within which each male has a circular territory 60 to 200 feet across. With whistling, stamping, and posturing, the male kob displays to and mates with any female that enters his particular field.* (Leonard Lee Rue III/ National Audubon Society Collection/Photo Researchers, Inc.)

48 *third overleaf. A zebra cannot be mistaken for any other creature, but within the three species of zebras—indeed, within the most widely distributed species, the plains zebra* (Equus burchelli)—*there is great variation in the striping. Zebras find a certain amount of safety from their chief nemesis, the lion, by mingling with large herds of other grazing animals—oryx, wildebeests, even ostriches. Their primary defense in an attack is speed—up to 40 miles an hour—but their hooves and teeth are weapons to make a lion wary.* (Erwin A. Bauer)

44 *overleaf. Weighing 1800 pounds and carrying five-foot horns, the African buffalo* (Syncerus caffer) *has a reputation—at least partly deserved—as the continent's most dangerous animal. Although it is normally peaceable, a wounded buffalo will lie in ambush for a hunter, and an old bull may stalk and charge a man without provocation. Oxpeckers are constantly in attendance on these wild cattle, ridding them of the torment of blood-sucking ticks.* (Bob and Jill Stoecker/Natura Photographica)

46 *second overleaf. A herd of blue wildebeests* (Connochaetes taurinus) *in flight across the Serengeti Plain of Tanzania. Widely dispersed during the rainy months, wildebeests gather in tremendous assemblages of hundreds of thousands in the dry season, moving forever about, single-file, seeking water and pasture. The wildebeest is a favorite prey of lions, hyenas, and wild dogs, and predators may claim eight out of every ten calves before they reach maturity.* (Thomas Nebbia)

On the Mediterranean coast of France, just west of Marseille, the two forks of the Rhone River flow to the sea in a welter of marshes, mudflats, and shallow lagoons. This vast delta region, known as the Camargue, is a land of beauty, strange and almost alien in aspect. Wild boars slosh through the shallows. Amphibians and reptiles swarm in freshwater marshes. Foxes skirt the salt lagoons where—astonishingly—vast flocks of greater flamingos congregate. And over this curious landscape roam herds of fierce black cattle and wild free horses, many almost white as snow.

The horses and cattle of the Camargue are domestic animals, but over long years they have been allowed to roam relatively free of interference, although the cattle, mostly privately owned, are branded and the horses are sometimes caught and broken as mounts for the herdsmen. For all purposes, the cattle and horses of the Camargue are feral, reverted to an untamed state and living much as their wild ancestors did in prehistoric times. They are a reminder of the close links between many domestic creatures and their wild forebears and of how recently, in the long course of mammalian evolution, man has shaped domestic breeds. The domestic horse, for instance, was bred from the wild horse *(Equus caballus)* which ranged the steppes of the Ukraine more than 5000 years ago. Domestic breeds undoubtedly were developed from a number of local, and now extinct, races. The only wild horses alive today are the zebras and the Mongolian horse *(E. c. przewalskii)*. The latter barely survives in the wild, and there is considerable thought that it may be a completely distinct

The Domesticated Ones

species from that which produced domestic horses. The horses of the Camargue, like the mustangs of the American West, are not wild in the strict sense, but actually are a domestic strain that has run free for 2000 years.

In the course of domestication, the traits that have made for manageability have been accentuated, and those that pose inconvenience or downright danger to humans have been eliminated by selective breeding. Thus it is that the male domestic yak *(Bos grunniens)* is half the size of its rare wild relative, which weighs more than a thousand pounds. Similarly, most donkeys are smaller than the pony-sized North African wild ass *(E. asinus)*, their graceful, fleet ancestor, and many strains of domestic water buffalo *(Bubalus bubalis)* are considerably less bulky than the wild variety, and have less imposing horns, sometimes none at all.

The water buffalo has been harnessed for use because of its adaptability to a very special set of environmental circumstances. It can be used for milk production, and more importantly as a beast of burden, in the hot, swampy places that are all but unlivable for domestic cattle and oxen. Because the water buffalo can work in the mud and water of rice paddies, marshes, and jungles, it has gained in numbers to perhaps 150 million animals worldwide. Water buffaloes have been spread to such diverse lands as Italy, Brazil, and Australia, running feral in parts of the latter two countries.

The same adaptability to quite special surroundings characterizes several other domestic ungulates. The yak, the llama *(Lama glama)*, and the alpaca *(L. pacos)* are all suited for the windswept reaches of the high mountains. All have been developed from beasts that evolved on arid tableland up to altitudes of 17,000 feet, and even higher in the case of the yak. The llama, a beast of burden, and the alpaca, kept for its long, fine wool, descend from the far-ranging guanaco *(L. guanicoe)*, which while it roams to the edge of the sea—and even to some islands—is very much a creature of the high, arid plains of the Andes. The yak's wild relative inhabits the wind-whipped deserts of northern Tibet, a bleak, barren wilderness. The country inhabited by these animals, and in which their domestic relatives are employed, represents some of the most difficult, dangerous terrain on earth, where surefootedness is at a premium and a capacity for subsisting on tough, sparse vegetation is essential. The shaggy winter coats that serve the guanaco and wild yak so well under near-glacial conditions have become in their domesticated relatives a source of extremely useful wool. Selective breeding, for example, has produced alpacas with fringes of wool so long they nearly brush the ground; the long, thin wool is considered to be among the world's finest and is extremely valuable.

The mountaineering abilities of the guanaco, its domestic descendants, and, for that matter, its close wild relative the vicuña, extend even to their metabolic processes. Their blood cells, small compared to those of humans, are numerous, providing a greater capacity to carry oxygen. Moreover, the hemoglobin in their blood has a relatively high affinity for oxygen, further boosting the talent these creatures have for operating under full speed at altitudes where exertion would leave many other animals gasping.

The guanaco, llama, alpaca, and vicuña belong to a family noted for its toughness and ability to get along under the most difficult conditions. The Old World members of the group, the camels, carry out the tradition in the deserts. Both of the two types of domestic camel can negotiate the most parched wastelands, the two-humped or Bactrian camel *(Camelus bactrianus)* where it is cold, the one-humped or dromedary *(C. dromedarius)* in regions where it is searingly hot. The endurance of the camel without water in the desert is legendary; the reasons for it are not fully understood. It seems, however, that the camel lasts so long without drinking because it uses water with nearly ultimate efficiency. Its urine is highly concentrated, but that is not particularly unique for desert animals. The camel, though, has other, rather unusual adaptations for living in the hot waterless places. Its woolly coat insulates it from the sun's heat. It can lower its body temperature during the cool desert night to as low as 90° F. It warms up slowly, and it is not until its body temperature exceeds 104° F. that it must begin to cool down. It can obtain water from its food, especially in the cooler winter when one can go months without drinking. Legends of water stored in the hump or stomach are untrue. For thousands of years—perhaps six thousand in the case of the dromedary—the camel's toughness and ability to withstand heat and lack of water have enabled the people who live with it to survive in regions that otherwise would not be populated by humans.

55 *and* **56** *overleaf. This young alpaca* (Lama pacos) *has been selectively bred for the long wool that will be sheared from its sides when it matures—a wool of unmatched quality that will be made into coats costing several thousand dollars. Once, garments of alpaca were worn only by Inca royalty. The alpaca and llama are domesticated forms of New World camels; two other kinds, the guanaco and vicuña, survive in a wild state in the South American Andes. The exact lineage of the alpaca and llama—indeed, even whether they should be considered true species—is a mystery that probably will plague science forever. Neither the alpaca nor the llama existed in the wild when the Spanish conquistadores arrived, and archaeological discoveries suggest they had been tamed and bred many centuries before the Inca Empire, probably from the wild guanaco. Moreover, all four New World camels interbreed and produce fertile offspring.* (55 Loren McIntyre; 56 George Holton/National Audubon Society Collection/Photo Researchers, Inc.)

58 *second overleaf. On a vast plateau 14,000 feet high in the Bolivian Andes, a herd of llamas* (Lama glama) *pauses to drink at a waterhole before taking on its cargo of salt.* (Loren McIntyre)

60-61. *The Altai Mountains rise in the distance as a herd of wild two-humped camels (Camelus bactrianus) crosses the Gobi Desert of Mongolia. There are two species of Old World camels, the one-humped dromedary, which originally came from Arabia, and the two-humped Bactrian camel from Chinese Turkestan and Mongolia. Both have been widely domesticated as beasts of burden, and only the Bactrian camel still survives in a wild population—numbering about*

900 animals on both sides of the
China-Mongolia border. In summer,
the wild camels climb into the
mountains as high as 11,000 feet
to escape the heat, returning to
the grassy steppes and desert in
winter. Heavy hunting for its
meat and hides, and competition
from domestic animals for scarce
water and pasture, are blamed for
the wild camel's decline. But this
rare species is now strictly
protected by both nations.
(George Holton)

62-63. *A herd of Indian wild asses* (Equus hemionus khur) *on the Little Rann of Kutch, a vast salt-impregnated wasteland near the Pakistan frontier. This is one of five subspecies of the Asiatic wild ass; one race, in Syria, is feared extinct, and all the others are considered rare. Competition from domestic livestock for badly over-grazed forage, uncontrolled slaughter for its meat and because its testes were thought to be a powerful aphrodisiac, and its capture for use as a draught animal exterminated the Indian wild ass from most of its historic range. But a thousand wild asses still survive on the Little Rann of Kutch, which lies only a foot or two above the Arabian Sea; there they have been rigorously protected for decades. Moreover, local people are strict vegetarians.* (Belinda Wright)

64 *overleaf. The only surviving race of truly wild horse is Przewalski's horse, which was once widely distributed across Asia. About two hundred of its kind are found in zoos around the world, and it is barely possible that a few still exist in the Gobi Desert of China and Mongolia. The so-called wild horses that range the western plains of North America are feral descendants of cowboys' steeds. And the Camargue horses that splash across the shallow lagoons of that marshy island on the Rhone delta of France likewise are domestic animals gone wild,* *although they are a fairly recent descendant of a wild horse that was crossed with Oriental blood.* (Hans Silvester/National Audubon Society Collection/Photo Researchers, Inc.)

High upon Kenya's Aberdare Mountains, towering almost 13,000 feet into the equatorial sky, lie rolling moorlands, swept by winds that play with the mist clouds and fray their edges to shreds. The air is cool, even chill, and the moors are laced with icy streams glistening under the roof of heaven. Scattered about the moors are outcrops of rock and, breaking up the expanses of low vegetation, thickets of giant heath, taller than a man and bearded with lichens. The gray-green vegetation of the thickets has a ravaged look, as if torn and splintered by some immensely powerful force. That, in fact, is exactly what has happened, for elephants climb the steep, slick trails into the highlands and feed in the foggy heath groves. Unable to jump, the elephants nevertheless are agile enough to climb the steep slopes that separate the moorlands from the forest below. Once they gain the top, they bulldoze into the thickets, white tusks gleaming amidst the dark foliage. The sight evokes images of Pleistocene times, some 50,000 years ago, when pachyderms roamed subglacial landscapes quite similar to the rolling uplands of the Aberdares. Largest living mammals outside the sea, the elephants serve as reminders that, in the Pleistocene, prodigious size was not uncommon among land mammals. In the world of nature, size is a signal advantage for a herbivorous creature; colossal bulk and the strength that goes with it can render a creature such as the elephant invulnerable to any land predator. But today the very size of the elephants and a few other giants has become a liability, because space is at a premium,

Unique Giants

especially where these giants live. With the possible exception of the giraffe *(Giraffa camelopardalis)*, the last giants have been pushed by expanding human populations into a few fragile havens in the jungles of Southeast Asia and the forests and grasslands of Africa. After existing unchanged for a million years, the Javan rhinoceros *(Rhinoceros sondaicus)* numbers no more than a score of animals clinging to life in a small reserve in Java and at best a handful roaming the backwaters of Indochina. The Sumatran rhino *(Didermocerus sumatrensis)* at one ton in weight the smallest of the giants, and heir to a line 40 million years old, is almost as rare. Perhaps less than 150 of these shaggy-eared forest rhinos survive, scattered through Southeast Asia. In the swampy grasslands and jungles of the Kaziranga National Park of Assam, India, and in the Royal Chitawan National Park of Nepal, live most of the world's 1200 great Indian rhinos. Like the Javan species, its close cousin, the Indian rhino *(R. unicornis)* is armored with heavy plates of thick skin, joined by thin folds that permit graceful, free movement. Given to frequent squabbles, Indian rhinos fight each other with slashing, and often fatal, swipes of incisors lengthened into razor-sharp tusks. The Indian rhino seldom employs its horn, which, as in other rhinos, is not a true horn with a bony core but is made of matted keratin fibers, like the material that forms a hoof. Perhaps because the Indian rhino prolongs its spectacularly violent mating act for the better part of an hour, rhino horn, from all species, is prized in Chinese folk medicine as an aphrodisiac, and sells for between

$1000 and $2000 a pound. This belief is unfortunate, for it makes rhinos a prime target for poachers. In most Oriental cities with large Chinese populations, one finds in medicine shops horn of rhinos from as far off as Africa. Both African rhinos, the black *(Diceros bicornis)* and the white or square-lipped *(Ceratotherium simum)*, carry two horns, which may reach a yard or more in length. Weighing more than 6000 pounds, the white rhino is the largest living rhinoceros, but a hornless rhino of about 30 million years ago towered twice as high and may have been the largest mammal ever to walk the earth.

Unlike the others, which feed mainly by browsing, the white rhinoceros is primarily a grazer and crops tough savanna grasses with the aid of the hard-edged upper lip of its squared-off snout. Two thousand miles divide the last two populations of white rhinos on earth, for of the few thousand left, some live on protected South African reserves, the others under questionable protection on the grasslands of Uganda, the northern Congo, and southern Sudan.

The windswept thorn scrub of Kenya and Tanzania is the heart of black rhino country, but this myopic beast inhabits several other regions scattered about sub-Saharan Africa. Tough as the whistling thorns among which it lives, the black rhino has a reputation for truculence, but this is partly the fault of its miserable eyesight, and often what appear to be thundering, snorting charges merely represent an attempt by the creature to take a close-up look. Surprised in the high grass, a black rhino like as not will face in the direction of an interloper, its piggy eyes squinting, the twitching of its nostrils wrinkling its snout above its prehensile upper lip, and ears flared. After a few moments, the rhino may wheel about and trot off. Then again, it may explode in a headlong charge.

More than 10,000 black rhinos live in Africa, but they depend almost entirely on sanctuaries, which they often share with the colossus among the giants, the African elephant *(Loxodonta africana)* of the bush country. A big bush elephant can reach six tons in weight and thirteen feet at the shoulder, twice the size of some members of the same species living in the green confines of the forest. When the need arises, the elephant can move its mountainous gray bulk over the ground at 25 miles an hour.

A slow-motion study in violence, the advance of an elephant herd eating its way through a grove of acacias in the African bush is unhurried but inexorable, and guaranteed to make a watcher feel puny, so casually do the great beasts commit acts of Herculean destruction. The elephants' great trunks, whose two-fingered tips are sensitive enough to pick up a peanut, gently wrap around sturdy tree limbs, then tear them away more easily than a man could pluck a rose. If leaves are too high, the trees that bear them are nudged by broad gray foreheads until wood splinters and they crash to the ground. An African elephant can consume up to 600 pounds of vegetation daily, so not surprisingly, when confined to parks, elephants literally eat themselves out of a home. Their destructive feeding has become an increasingly critical problem in Africa. Elongated upper incisors that grow throughout life, the tusks can reach a length of a dozen feet in African elephants. Although nominally outlawed, killing of elephants for their tusks goes on in most of their African range, with the ivory going to markets in Hong Kong and mainland China. Of itself, the poaching might not imperil the existence of the species, but in the face of declining habitat, the African elephant cannot long endure the poisoned arrows and traps of poachers.

The slightly smaller Asiatic elephant *(Elephas maximus)* also suffers severely from the constriction of its habitat, but in Asia, where wild elephants have been trained as beasts of burden for 5000 years, they seem more adaptable to life surrounded by people. Asiatic elephants, moreover, are not nearly as persecuted by ivory hunters, because they have much smaller tusks.

The hippopotamus *(Hippopotamus amphibius)* of Africa also carries formidable tusks, which are not incisors but canines in the lower jaw. When angered, the hippo open its jaws in a cavernous yawn, baring its huge weapons, which it can wield with lethal effectiveness. Most of the time, however, hippos are the picture of luxuriant loafing, particularly during the day. Bunched together in the mud like hogs, they bask on sandbanks, their dark hides tinged red by protective mucus, secreted by glands in the skin. Or else they float just breaking the surface of quiet water, an activity for which their eyes, ears, and nostrils are suitably positioned atop the snout and head.

Although the Indian rhino excels as a swimmer, and elephants revel in bathing, none of the giants is as aquatic as the hippo, which even is born underwater. Able to walk on the bottom, the hippo can stay under for up to six minutes.

After dark, however, the hippo is transformed. It heaves its body from the water and, leaving its platter-sized, four-toed prints in the mud, briskly heads overland. Along age-old trails, hippos may travel miles to their feeding plots. In the course of a night, 100 pounds of grass and other fodder can disappear down the maw of a single large hippo. If farmers have planted crops on hippo feeding grounds, the devastation is swift, and so is the reprisal. The last terrestrial giants have no way of knowing that they evolved in a world when humans were scattered and few, and no plow had broken the earth. They cannot know that the days when they were lords of the land are over, and that their fate is now entirely in the hands of a pygmy called man.

71. *When a bull hippopotamus* (Hippopotamus amphibius) *opens its cavernous mouth in a "yawn," exposing sharp incisors and huge lower canine tusks that may be twenty-five inches long, it is not a sign of laziness. By showing off the formidable weapons that jut from its powerful jaws, the hippo is trying to intimidate a rival. But such threat displays as often as not incite rather than prevent fights, and a battle between two hippos can be awesome and bloody. For an hour or two the hippos rush at each other with gaping mouths, sending waves rushing across the lake or river as they attempt to drive those great canine teeth—once used to make human dentures—through the thick hide and into the heart of their opponent.* (Robert Harrington)

72 *overleaf. A single horn and thickly folded, tubercle-covered skin that gives it an armored appearance identify the great Indian rhinoceros* (Rhinoceros unicornis). *Only a few hundred individuals of this endangered giant still survive in sanctuaries in India and Nepal. Weighing two and a half tons, the great Indian rhinoceros is the second largest of the five species of rhino found in Africa and Asia. The female bears a single calf after a gestation period of sixteen months, and the newborn rhino weighs 140 pounds and has all the skin folds and rivetlike protuberances of an adult, lacking only the nose horn. Over its first year of life, drinking twenty-five quarts of milk a day from its mother, the calf will multiply its weight tenfold at the rate of six pounds a day. It will not be weaned until it is two and a half years old.* (Belinda Wright)

76 *overleaf.* *With its hind feet reaching ahead of the front feet and its long neck swinging like a pendulum, the giraffe* (Giraffa camelopardalis) *can lope tirelessly across the East African plains at speeds of up to 30 miles an hour. Running is the giraffe's primary defense against its only natural enemy, the lion, but if cornered it can crush the big cat's skull with blows from its front legs.* (Wolfgang Bayer)

74-75. *Worrying the desiccated remains of one of its own, ripping apart an acacia tree to obtain part of the 300 pounds of food it requires every day, bathing with dust—all are routines in the daily life of the* African elephant (Loxodonta africana), *the largest land mammal on earth. In particular, elephants spend a great deal of time washing, powdering, and massaging their skin, which is unusually sensitive for a beast that weighs six tons.* (74 top John Reader; 74 bottom Sven Lindblad/National Audubon Society Collection/Photo Researchers, Inc.; 75 ANIMALS ANIMALS/© Jan Thiede)

Although many mammals roam the world's high places, one group of horned, hoofed creatures in particular has made the windswept, stony heights its special playground. Native in one form or another to Eurasia, northern Africa, and North America, the goats, sheep, and a few related beasts clatter over all but the very highest reaches of the mountains with a wild freedom that makes them seem kin to the wind. Superbly equipped for life atop the crags, these mountaineering mammals feed, breed, and even rear their young on landscapes of incredible harshness. The four-chambered stomachs of these ruminants can glean enough nourishment from rubbery scrub, wisps of grass, and scraps of lichen to thrive in the marginal environment of the peaks, where other large mammals would starve. For example, the mouflon *(Ovis musium)*, wild sheep of the Mediterranean, can subsist even on the plant known as deadly nightshade.

Amazingly sure of foot, these creatures of the alpine solitudes have a dizzying aptitude for cavorting on eminences above the clouds. Persian wild goats *(Capra hircus)* leap about the boulders almost 14,000 feet up in the barren mountains west of the Caspian Sea, where Iran, the Soviet Union, and Turkey meet. The big Siberian ibex *(C. ibex sibirica)* goes even higher and, like others of its species, easily perches on any pinnacle with enough room for its four feet. Bighorn sheep *(Ovis canadensis)* survey the Rocky Mountains from lookouts 10,000 feet high. In the Himalayas, blue sheep *(Pseudois nayaur)*—not exactly true sheep and not blue, either, but gray—loll on grassy slopes at 18,000 feet.

Life on the Peaks

Of them all, however, the true king of the mountain is the North American mountain goat *(Oreamnos americanus)*, a bearded will-o'-the-wisp as white as the snow that swirls about its native western mountains in the winter. Once sighted in the heights, the goats are given to vanishing with ghostly abruptness, then suddenly reappearing at the edge of even higher peaks. The mountain goat is not a true goat, but along with its cousins the Eurasian chamois, and the serows, gorals, and takins of Asia, is classified as a goat antelope, because it possesses traits of both. Scientists have trouble classifying some of the mountaineering mammals. The blue sheep, for instance, is not quite a sheep, and not a goat, but a little like both, so in the end its name is based upon its general appearance.

The backgrounds against which the mountain goat is pictured tell much about the brutal conditions with which it must cope. Unlike the bighorns, which descend to the shelter of lower slopes in the autumn, and the corkscrew-horned markhor goats *(Capra falconieri)* of Asia, which emerge from the heights to feed on live oak when the snow flies, the mountain goats seldom stray below the timberline. There are exceptions, of course, but mountain goats generally head for the trees only in the spring, when the sweet, green shoots lure them from their high havens. The goats negotiate the steep slopes and sheer, gray headwalls of their world with stiff-legged deliberation, pausing frequently to consider the next move. Traveling this way a goat can ascend nearly vertical palisades, when necessary pulling its 300-pound body from ledge to ledge with its black forefeet. If a goat reaches a dead-end ledge, it rears upon its hind legs, whirls about, and returns the way it came, often by stupendous leaps from rock to rock. The fancy footwork of the goat is due in large measure to the structure of its hooves; it and the other members of the group have two on each foot. In the center of each hoof is a spongy, elastic pad, like a tire tread, which provides traction, while the hard-edged rim of the hoof catches in minute clefts and crevices—an arrangement shared by other mountain mammals.

The chamois *(Rupicapra rupicapra)*, which roves mountain ranges from the Pyrenees to the Caucasus, and has been transplanted to New Zealand, is more graceful than its American relative. But it has the same uncanny ability to materialize seemingly out of nowhere. One moment a talus slope appears empty, the next a chamois is there, scanning the slopes below.

If it senses danger, however, the chamois moves with dazzling speed, leaping and bounding over chasms so lightly it seems to fly. If cornered, a chamois fights with vicious thrusts of its foot-long horns, but rarely are these weapons used so murderously as in rutting battles between the males.

Chamois, and mountain goats, sometimes fight to the death in such combats, and once the weaker duelist gives ground, he may be pursued ferociously, even knocked spinning from a cliff. Male mountain goats, moreover, do not reserve their aggressiveness for other adult males, but are notorious kid killers, perhaps the worst enemies of their own young.

The rutting combats of most other animals in this group, on the other hand, are ritualized to prevent serious injury and death. The crash of bighorns hammering against each other's huge, curled horns sometimes can be heard a mile away—but the blows are always horn on horn. The horns also armor their owners against even pile-driving blows, which also are cushioned by the skull. Bighorns have a tendency, like an experienced boxer, to "roll with the punch." Males with horns markedly different in size seldom fight.

The males of most of the true sheep and goats carry horns that are massive in relation to their body size. The Nubian ibex, found in Israel and the Sinai, as well

s Africa, has horns almost four feet long. Yet this
smallest of ibexes is not much more than knee-high to a
man at its shoulder. The Persian wild goat, which
weighs less than 100 pounds, has saber-shaped horns
that sometimes reach a length of more than five feet.
And even a mouflon, little more than two feet high at
the shoulder, can have horns a yard long.
The most impressive horns of all, however, belong to the
argali sheep *(Ovis ammon)*, an awesome creature four
feet high at the shoulder, larger than a bighorn. Some
argalis carry horns that, flaring outward in a wide
spiral, approach six feet from tip to tip. The argalis
inhabit some of the bleakest mountains in the world,
in the cold interior of central Asia, and in their
isolation are symbolic of all the mountain animals, for
they are creatures of a world that, until recently,
existed on a plane above humanity. As long as the
mountaineering mammals remain in the wild, they are
assurance that somewhere on this earth, a living
creature remains in splendid isolation.

83. *A Dall sheep ram (Ovis dalli) snorts a warning. Wild mountain sheep—rams in particular—are customarily silent animals, but on their summer pasture the ewes and lambs in a herd carry on a noisy conversation that suggests a flock of domestic sheep. This species is named for the American naturalist William Healey Dall, who was a student of Louis Agassiz and one of the first scientists to explore Alaska at the time of its purchase from Russia by the United States.* (Gary Milburn/TOM STACK & ASSOCIATES)

84 *overleaf. The white coat of the Dall sheep harmonizes with its chosen home—the snowy mountain heights of Alaska and northwestern Canada. This is a summer bachelors' club of rams of all ages, for they play no role in the raising of lambs. But such peaceful coexistence will end in late autumn, when jealous competition for the attention of ewes is renewed. The slender, flaring horns of Dall sheep contrast with the massive, tightly curled horns of the bighorn sheep that claim the Rocky Mountains to the south.* (Stephen J. Krasemann/DRK Photo)

86 *second overleaf. A sifting of hard snow crystals salts the face of a 300-pound Rocky Mountain bighorn ram (Ovis canadensis) during a subzero snowstorm. The chips in his huge horns are the scars of head-butting battles, and the horn tips are splintered from violent clashes with other big rams. The deep creases were formed each autumn when the horns temporarily stopped growing, and the segments between the creases represent the twelve years of his life. The annual growth gets smaller as the ram grows older, and this monarch is nearing retirement, for few bighorns live beyond the age of fourteen.* (James K. Morgan)

88 *third overleaf. The master of a harem of bighorn ewes routs a young rival. Negotiating such precipitous cliffs is not a great challenge for a mountain sheep. Its hoof has a hard outer edge and toe that grips in loose dirt or rock cracks, plus a resilient pad at the back that provides traction on smooth surfaces. Moreover, to the ram's eye there usually are well-defined, if zigzag, paths across such jagged rock faces. And if not, the bighorn can plunge down a rock chute, hurtling from niche to niche in a controlled fall with the ease that comes from superb traction and balance.* (Harry Engels)

90 *fourth overleaf. Fights between two male ibex (Capra ibex) are spectacular affairs, but they are usually only ritualized play between two peers rather than serious combat for domination of a harem. Rising on their hind legs, these bearded wild goats will clatter their four-foot-long, saberlike horns together; or they will wrestle with horns hooked, pushing with their foreheads. Ibex dwell high in the mountains of Eurasia and northern Africa, browsing alpine meadows and resting in the shade of rock overhangs. They were nearly exterminated throughout much of their range because superstitious people—as late as the nineteenth century—believed that their horns, blood, heart muscles—even their feces—could cure countless ailments. But the ibex has been successfully reintroduced in many parts of the Alps.* (René Pierre Bille)

92 *fifth overleaf. The highest crags of North America's highest mountains are where the mountain goat (Oreamnos americanus) is likely to be found in summer. There, far above the haunts of traditional enemies—wolves, grizzly bears, cougars—the nanny and her one or two kids are safe from all enemies but soaring golden eagles. And it is a rare event when one of the huge raptors succeeds in carrying off a kid. As winter approaches, and the mountain goat descends to forested valleys to escape deep snows, it acquires a heavy coat six to eight inches long on top of a four-inch layer of woolly underfur.* (Antje Gunnar/TOM STACK & ASSOCIATES)

Notes on Photographers

Erwin A. Bauer (48) has worked as a freelance photographer in northern California since 1948. He is the author of *Living Water* and *Tideline*.

Wolfgang Bayer (76) is a wildlife film producer who has made television films for the National Geographic Society, Walt Disney Productions, and *Wild World of Animals*.

René Pierre Bille (90) is a Swiss naturalist and film maker who is especially interested in wild animals of the Alps.

Stanley Breeden (19) has photographed wildlife throughout the world. His pictures have been published in numerous international publications.

John Burnley (25) lives on Long Island, New York, and has photographed in the Arctic and Alaska.

Thase Daniel (15), a native of Arkansas, has photographed wildlife in remote parts of many countries. Her photographs have appeared in numerous books and magazines.

Harry Engels (88) photographs wildlife of the northern Rockies. His articles and pictures have appeared in many publications.

Francisco Erize (42) lives in Argentina and has photographed wildlife in South American jungles, the Galápagos and Antarctica.

Jean-Paul Ferrero (18) is a French wildlife photographer whose work has been published in numerous European books and periodicals.

Gary Griffen (20) photographs scenics and animals of the Hudson Valley and Catskill Mountains.

Antje Gunnar (92), a mountaineer and world traveler, has had photographs in *International Wildlife* and in National Geographic Books.

Robert Harrington (71) is a photographer for the Michigan Department of Natural Resources. His pictures have appeared in numerous publications, including *National Geographic*.

George Holton (56, 60) was a New York based photographer whose work appeared in publications of the National Audubon Society, the National Geographic Society and Time-Life Books. His travels took him to nearly every part of the world.

M. Philip Kahl's (38) work has been reproduced in many magazines and books. Grants from the National Geographic Society have aided his study of storks and flamingos of the world.

Russ Kinne (39) is a veteran freelance natural history photographer and the author of *The Complete Book of Nature Photography*.

Dean Krakel II (22) lives in Oklahoma City and specializes in wildlife portraiture and general photojournalism.

Stephen J. Krasemann's (84) photographs have appeared in numerous wildlife periodicals, books and calendars.

Sven Lindblad (74) was born in Sweden but now lives in the United States. He has photographed throughout the world, particularly in East Africa, the Arctic and Antarctica.

Loren McIntyre (55, 58) is a writer, photographer and film maker. His subjects are South American, with emphasis on the Andes and the Amazon.

Gary Milburn (83) specializes in photographing the wildlife of South America. He works for the Environmental Protection Agency.

James K. Morgan (86) is a wildlife biologist who spent eight years studying and writing about bighorn sheep. His photographs have appeared in *Audubon* and *National Geographic*.

Thomas Nebbia (2, 46) freelances for *National Geographic*, mainly in Germany. Born in Rochester, New York, he now lives in Copenhagen.